A PLAY IN ONE ACT

A POINT OF VIEW

by

DAVID CAMPTON

D0869658

THE DRAMATIC PUBLISHING COMPANY

A POINT OF VIEW
A Play in One Act
For Five Women

CHARACTERS

AUNTIE

BETTY

LOUISE

MIRIAM

FLORENCE

TIME: *Present.*

PLACE: *Auntie's room.*

A POINT OF VIEW

SCENE: Auntie's room. The set is angled to show
two walls. The corner appears RC so the right
wall is shorter than the left. There is a large
window in the left wall, and auntie's bed is
pushed against the window, and along the wall.
The bed has a bookcase headboard and on the
shelf is a telephone. At the head of the bed is
a locker, and beside the locker, a chair. Another
chair stands at the foot of the bed. The door to
the room is DR.)

AT RISE OF CURTAIN: AUNTIE is sitting up in
bed. She is looking down into the street through
a pair of binoculars.)

AUNTIE. Ah-ha! (She puts down the binoculars,
and writes in a large book.) "Ten forty-five.
Mrs. Knee meets Mrs. Scan on the pawnbroker's
corner. They talk. They smile." . . . That's
a nasty smile. It means -- I know something
about you that you don't know I know. They're
both smiling. It must be an interesting conversation down there. Why did I never learn lip-
reading? (She thumps with a stick on the floor.
She starts turning back pages of the book.) Now
let's see . . . it would be about a week last
Tuesday. . . . Ah. (Reading.) "Thursday, the
twenty-fifth. Seven-fifteen. Mr. Scan meets
Mrs. Knee on the pawnbroker's corner. They
shake hands. Mr. Scan forgets to let go. They

5

walk slowly toward town. . . . Showing at the
Roxy "Naked Passion" in Naturama. "

(The door opens and BETTY CHARLES comes in.)

BETTY. You were knocking again.

AUNTIE. You get slower, Betty Charles. What is
it -- old age?

BETTY. The boss doesn't like it.

AUNTIE. She can please herself. It's a free
country. Listen, Betty . . .

BETTY. Lucky for you I'd just put a customer under
the drier. If I'd been shampooing . . .

AUNTIE. I'd have knocked again. Nip out to the
sweet shop, will you?

BETTY. The boss says it's got to stop.

AUNTIE. Ask for a quarter of peppermints -- the
sort that take the top of your head off.

BETTY. She says I'm paid to be a hairdresser's
assistant, not an old girl's errand boy.

AUNTIE. And at the same time find out if the Scan
youngsters have been in with their Saturday
pennies.

BETTY. She says I encourage you, and if she catches
me here again, she'll tear me up in long, thin
strips.

AUNTIE. If they haven't, ask -- casually -- if they've
been sent to their Gran's in the country.

BETTY. You don't want me to be torn up in long,
thin strips, do you?

AUNTIE. And if you cross over by the pawnbroker's
corner, catch a few words of what's being said.

BETTY. You're not listening.

AUNTIE. It saves time to carry on two conversations
at once. What are you waiting for?

BETTY. I could lose my job.

AUNTIE. You won't.

BETTY. The boss . . .

AUNTIE. I know Louie. Run along.

BETTY. Why do you want to know about the Scans?

AUNTIE. That's my business.

BETTY. It's called blackmail.

AUNTIE. What is?

BETTY. What you do with what you find out.

AUNTIE. Call it manipulation.

BETTY. I'd better get back to the shop. I couldn't be all this time looking for clean towels.

AUNTIE. I could do something for you.

BETTY. What?

AUNTIE. I owe you something for running up and down stairs. Don't you want me to help you?

BETTY. How can you?

AUNTIE. You've got your eye on a boy, haven't you?

BETTY. Who hasn't?

AUNTIE. I haven't. But you're young, and your third finger's aching for a ring. . . . His name's Charlie, isn't it? A spineless five-foot-ten, with too much oil on too much hair. He works at Forges Motors from Monday to Friday, and hangs around the Palais every Saturday.

BETTY. How did? . . . Anyway, he's engaged to the blonde from the chemists'.

AUNTIE. Not after last night. And don't ask me how I know because I shan't tell you. But you be at the Palais tonight in your best bib and tucker; pounce, and you've got him. He'll be lonely tonight.

BETTY. You're a witch.

AUNTIE. That's called thanks. . . . And when you've opened his eyes to the fact that you're alive and feminine, suggest moving over to The Cormorant Club. Charlie's ambitious -- The Cormorant's a step up. Ask for Fred Boot and tell him Auntie sent you. If Charlie isn't yours by the time you

kiss good night, you don't know how to play
your cards.

BETTY. How do you do it -- wax figures and pins?

AUNTIE. A lot of people would like to know. But,
look, Betty. What do you see from the window?

BETTY. Just people.

AUNTIE. It's useful having a bed on the first floor,
because I can see further. With my binoculars
I can look right into their faces. For instance,
Mrs. Scan and Mrs. Knee are still smiling.
Fancy, keeping up a smile as long as that with-
out letting it quiver. . . . Here's a telephone
keeping me in touch with other people out of
sight. I keep a diary. Here it is; all the facts
in date order. I lie back, and put two and two
together. From little bits of knowledge I make
bigger bits of knowledge. Then I find people who
know what I want to know, and I pay for what
they know with what I know. That way I make
my knowledge grow.

BETTY. It's spooky.

AUNTIE. By the way, you'll keep your eyes open at
The Cormorant Club, won't you? Knowledge,
you know. Every little helps.

BETTY. It won't help me if I get the push for coming
up to you.

AUNTIE. You won't get the push.

BETTY. Promise.

AUNTIE. That's a promise.

(Door opens and LOUISE strides in.)

LOUISE. Betty Charles.

BETTY. Yes, Miss Louise.

LOUISE. You're fired.

BETTY. Yes, Miss Louise.

AUNTIE. The name is Scan. S-C-A-N. Find out

what you can. (BETTY goes out, shutting the
door after her.) Good of you to drop in, Louie.
The telephone's all very well, but it lacks that
personal touch.

LOUISE. You knew my mother. That is all we have
in common.

AUNTIE. What a woman! Splendid eye for detail.

LOUISE. Trading on that friendship, you were
allowed to occupy the flat over my salon.

AUNTIE. At an exorbitant rent, if I may say so.

LOUISE. You don't pay it.

AUNTIE. My nieces do. It's in the family.

LOUISE. A woman comes in four times a day to
prepare meals and make your bed. Your
nieces pay for that, too. Not an ideal arrange-
ment. An old person's home would be much
more satisfactory.

AUNTIE. I'm independent. (Looks down into the
street.) Don't mind me using the binoculars.

LOUISE. Living alone was all very well when you
had full use of your faculties.

AUNTIE. Mrs. Knee has dropped her smile. . . .
Smack. Smack. Now the case is public property.

LOUISE. Understand?

AUNTIE. Quite. You want to be rid of me. (Writing
in her diary.) "Mrs. Scan and Mrs. Knee fight.
Mrs. Knee struck the first blow."

LOUISE. You must find somewhere else to live.

AUNTIE. I'm sorry, Louie. I like to be helpful.
But where would I find another window like this?
Overlooking a main thoroughfare with a pawnbroker's on one corner, a pub on the other, and
a betting shop in between. You'll just have to
put up with me for a few more years until I'm
wheeled away.

LOUISE. I can be obstinate, too.

AUNTIE. You're not fighting me, are you?

LOUISE. You are an interfering old harridan who
    is damaging my business. I want you out.
    Continue the story from there.
AUNTIE. I can't understand what men see in you,
    Louie.
LOUISE. Men?
AUNTIE. After all, you're no chicken, and you've
    a bite like an east wind.
LOUISE. What did you mean by "men"?
AUNTIE. The same as you. Growling creatures in
    trousers who pay for the drinks. I hear you
    have a collection. At least the graying civil
    servant who dined at The Boar was different
    from the young spark who reserved a table at
    the Country Club. Do they know each other?
LOUISE. You're a . . . a . . .
AUNTIE. Give yourself time to think. . . . Betty
    won't be handed her cards at the end of the
    week, will she?
LOUISE. I won't be blackmailed.

(Door opens and BETTY hurries in breathlessly.)

BETTY. One quarter of strong mints. The little
    Scans were sent into the country last night. One
    lady said "Cow," and the other said "Bitch."
    Oh, are you still here, Miss Louise?
AUNTIE. She was explaining about your job, Betty.
    You'll still be with us after next week.
BETTY. Oh, thank you, Miss Louise.
LOUISE. Get . . . downstairs.
BETTY. Yes, Miss Louise. (She goes out, leaving
    the door open.)
LOUISE. You'll go. I promise you that. You'll go.
    (She goes out, slamming the door behind her.)
AUNTIE (looking out of the window). Hm. (Writes.)
    "Ten fifty-two. Mrs. Scan and Mrs. Knee parted

by policewoman. " . . . Now where does that
fit in?

(The lights are lowered to denote the passing of
time. When they come up, AUNTIE is on
the telephone.)

AUNTIE. . . . Ah-ha. . . . Oh, it won't last,
Polly. There's a difference between holding
hands in the back row of "Naked Passion," and
facing each other in the raw light of morning.
The question is -- will the Scan family take him
back when the fire goes out? Leave that one to
me, Polly.

(Door opens and MIRIAM and FLO come in.)

MIRIAM. Auntie, darling!
FLO. Afternoon, Auntie.
AUNTIE (into telephone). Visitors.
MIRIAM. Oh. Sssh.
FLO. Sorry.
AUNTIE (into telephone). Only my nieces. Reading
from left to right, Miriam and Florence. I'll
ring back later. Good-bye, Polly. (She replaces
the receiver.)
MIRIAM. I brought a bag of grapes for you -- the
little green sour ones you like so much.
FLO. And I brought a couple of peaches. They're
hard, but that means they'll keep longer.
AUNTIE. Thank you, Florence. Thank you,
Miriam. Now sit down and tell me what you
want. Well?
MIRIAM (clearing her throat). Well . . .
AUNTIE. Yes?
FLO. Yes.
MIRIAM. I . . .

FLO. We . . . (Pause.)

AUNTIE. I take my castor oil neat.

MIRIAM. You know we're very fond of you, Auntie.
    You mean so much to us. So very, very much.

FLO. To both of us.

AUNTIE. When the gumsucking and toothtasting's
    out of the way, tell me what you want.

FLO. You're to come and live with us.

AUNTIE. Is that an invitation or an order?

MIRIAM. You should know Flo by now, Auntie,
    dear. She always wanted to be a quartermaster-
    sergeant. She drills those children of hers like
    guardsmen.

FLO. At least mine are growing up to be boys, and
    not sausages.

AUNTIE. That's more like yourselves. For a while
    I was afraid you were in a decline.

MIRIAM. What Flo meant to say was this . . .

FLO. Behind the gush Miriam is repeating what I
    said in the first place. You're to live with us.

AUNTIE. No, thank you.

MIRIAM. So convenient -- even Flo agreed to it.
    You'll have your own little room, with me to
    wait on you hand and foot.

AUNTIE. I've been at your mercy before, Miriam.
    I can forgive, but I can't forget.

MIRIAM. You need never be lonely -- the twins
    always pattering in and out . . .

FLO. You'll be properly cared for with me. To
    start with a no-nonsense diet.

AUNTIE. Yeast powder, dried milk, and black
    molasses.

FLO. You'll soon settle down.

MIRIAM. We owe so much to you, Auntie, dear.
    I told Flo as much over coffee when we met to
    thrash . . . to come to this agreement. I said
    we must make sure that Auntie's twilight years

    are taken care of.

AUNTIE. I said no.

FLO. It's a duty. I've never been one to shirk
    duties. Wilfred agrees, of course.

AUNTIE. Miriam.

MIRIAM. Yes, Auntie?

AUNTIE. Look me in the eye. . . . In the eye,
    not past my left ear. What are you hiding?

MIRIAM. Don't let this be one of your difficult
    days, Auntie.

FLO. I warned you she'd be awkward.

MIRIAM. I tried to make everything sound abso-
    lutely enchanting, darling. And, honestly,
    it only needs the slightest adjustment on your
    part, and we'll all be as happy as . . . as
    mayflies.

FLO. I warned you to stick to the facts, but, no
    . . . you must have your fancy wrapping.

AUNTIE. What are the facts?

FLO. Six months with Miriam. Six months with
    me.

MIRIAM. It's the best we can do.

FLO. It's the most we can afford.

MIRIAM. Now the rent is to be doubled.

AUNTIE. Wait, now . . .

MIRIAM. We don't blame Louise. After all, this
    place would fetch even more if it were given a
    coat of paint and decent wallpaper. So near to
    the shops. (AUNTIE picks up the telephone and
    dials.) Though, when we talked the matter
    over, we realized what sillies we must have
    been all these years.

FLO. It will be cheaper to have you with us.

MIRIAM. And it will be no trouble. None at all.
    So banish all those little worries from your
    mind.

AUNTIE (into telephone). Louie? . . . Come up

here. . . . I don't care what you're in the
middle of. Leave the woman's head to soak and
come up here. At once. (Slams down receiver.)

MIRIAM. And, Auntie, dear, imagine all the
goodies the saving will buy you -- tonic wine,
chicken broth, calvesfoot jelly . . .

AUNTIE. Slippery elm and arrowroot.

MIRIAM. It will be such fun, darling. The twins
are talking about it already. Imagine their
bursting in to greet you every morning.

AUNTIE. I shall take to drink.

FLO. Not in my house. You need nourishing milk.
Make a new woman of you.

AUNTIE. There'll be little enough left of the old
one. Which of you is to have the pleasure of
incarcerating me first?

MIRIAM. Well . . .

FLO. Actually . . .

AUNTIE. Those are the first encouraging words
this afternoon.

MIRIAM. We haven't had time to work out every
little detail.

AUNTIE. As long as there's an area of disagree-
ment . . . whoever has me first, has me for
Christmas; whoever has me second, has me
for the summer holidays.

FLO. One of us will have to make sacrifices.

AUNTIE. I pin my hopes to that.

(LOUISE comes in.)

AUNTIE. Congratulations, Louie. You're a fast
worker.

LOUISE. I thought you'd appreciate the tactics. Is
everything decided?

AUNTIE. Not quite.

FLO. But it will be.

AUNTIE. Good-bye, girls.

MIRIAM. But we've only just arrived.

AUNTIE. You said what you came to say. The
    message registered. Besides, I have some-
    thing to say to Louie that you're too young to
    overhear. Give my love to the twins, Miriam.
    Here's a present for them -- a couple of peaches.
    Pity they're not ripe, but they keep longer that
    way. And here's something for your boys, Flo
    -- a bag of green grapes -- full of vitamins.
    You can kiss me good-bye.

FLO (kissing AUNTIE). There, Auntie.

MIRIAM (kissing AUNTIE). There, Auntie.

AUNTIE. Oh, Miriam . . . (Whispers to her.)

MIRIAM (in a loud whisper). I understand, Auntie.

AUNTIE. Good-bye, now.

FLO (grimly). Good-bye.

MIRIAM. Good-bye, Auntie. (She takes FLO's arm
    and urges her out, shutting the door behind
    them.)

LOUISE. That's the situation. What more is there
    to say?

AUNTIE. Sssh. I'm waiting for Flo.

(FLO returns, and shuts the door behind her.)

FLO. You whispered to Miriam.

AUNTIE. I knew that would bring you back. I wanted
    a word with you alone. See me tomorrow after-
    noon. Without Miriam. It's important. Now go
    back to her quickly, or she'll want to know what
    you've been told. (FLO goes, and shuts the door
    behind her.)

LOUISE. It won't work -- whatever you're plotting.

AUNTIE. Don't go into the chicken business, Louie;
    you'll never get your books to balance. . . .
    Isn't that Mrs. Scan down there? (Looks through

her binoculars.) Tarted up like yesterday's
leftover. I'd say she wanted the man back.
. . . What did you say, Louie?

LOUISE. I'll have these rooms done over.

AUNTIE. About time, too.

LOUISE. I know a . . . businessman prepared to
take them . . . at my price.

AUNTIE. Is he prepared to take me with them?

LOUISE. You've taken a fall this time, Auntie.
I'd be sorry for you if I weren't so glad. (She
goes out. AUNTIE picks up the telephone and
dials. While she waits for a reply, she looks
out the window.)

AUNTIE. Two boys with cap pistols, shooting it out
around the green grocer's barrels. Why aren't
they in school? . . . (Into telephone.) . . . Is that
you, Polly? Poll, I'm worried. Suppose I'm
losing my touch? I'm worried . . .

(The lights are lowered to denote the passing of time.
When the lights come up, AUNTIE is sitting
back with her eyes shut, her diary on her chest.
There is a knock at the door, and BETTY comes
in.)

AUNTIE (opening her eyes). Miriam? . . . Oh, it's
you, Betty. I didn't knock for you.

BETTY. It's my tea-break. She can't stop me coming
up on my tea-break. She says you're moving.

AUNTIE. Always check your facts. You know how
rumors get spread. I didn't say I was moving.
Peppermint?

BETTY. No, thanks. I tried one when I fetched
them from the sweetshop. Want the news? The
Scan boys came back from their Gran's this
morning.

AUNTIE. I know.

BETTY. Your network must be on overtime.

AUNTIE. That's right.

BETTY. I'll tell you something you don't know, then.

AUNTIE. You had a raise today.

BETTY. You are a witch. It ought not to be legal. Even I didn't know till a minute ago. She told me to keep it to myself. She didn't tell you?

AUNTIE. I put two and two together. Did Charlie fall for The Cormorant Club? Two and two usually make four.

BETTY. That doesn't make sense.

AUNTIE. Don't argue with mathematics. You're sure you didn't recognize anybody at The Cormorant?

BETTY. Not a soul. It's all very well for a lark, but I'll be back at the Palais tomorrow. I know when I'm out of my depth.

AUNTIE. You can keep your head above water. Was it a good raise?

BETTY. You mean there's something you don't know?

AUNTIE. I'm always ready to learn.

BETTY. Ten bob. I can start saving regular now.

AUNTIE. Going steady?

BETTY. I'll tell you that at the right time. Some things ought to be kept private. Why do you do it, anyway -- the binoculars, the telephone, the questions, the gossip -- what's it all for?

AUNTIE. I want to live. That's simple enough, isn't it? I'm running short of time. I want to make the most of the scraps while they last. I want to be everywhere and know everything. I can't because I'm . . . I'm limited . . . to this room and this view. . . . All right, so I'm an interfering busybody. But, if you found a couple of ends hanging loose, wouldn't you be tempted

to tie them together? Send me a slice of the
wedding cake. In the meantime, don't take too
many chances with Charlie.

BETTY. Charlie? Oh, the boy.

(MIRIAM flutters in.)

MIRIAM. Auntie, darling, the traffic! Really, I'd
have been faster in a wheelbarrow.

BETTY. My tea must be getting cold.

AUNTIE. Come up again when you have something
to tell me.

BETTY. Tell you something now, Auntie. Your
crystal ball needs a polish.

AUNTIE. Really?

BETTY. His name isn't Charlie. (She goes out,
and shuts the door behind her.)

AUNTIE. Sharp girl. Pity that brother of mine
couldn't have produced a daughter like her.

MIRIAM. In which case she would have been your
niece.

AUNTIE. So she would.

MIRIAM. I'm your niece.

AUNTIE. Good morning, Miriam.

MIRIAM. Now, what can I do for you?

AUNTIE. Do? I take it you've discussed my future
with Flo again.

MIRIAM. My dear, one never discusses anything
with Flo. One merely listens to the same tired
argument again and again and again. If she
weren't my sister, I'd call her pig-headed.

AUNTIE. So you haven't settled who's to have me
first. . . . You're a generous girl, Miriam.

MIRIAM. I know. It's a terrible disadvantage.

AUNTIE. I want to ask a favor.

MIRIAM. Anything, sweetie.

AUNTIE. I want to stay with Florence first.

MIRIAM. Auntie!

AUNTIE. When you're ready to listen, I'll explain.
In the meantime, pass the binoculars.

MIRIAM (handing binoculars to AUNTIE). Not that I
give a . . . a pig's whistle for summer holidays.
Holidays come and go. When they're finished,
they're done with; nothing left but a tan that fades
as soon as you look at it. But to hear you say that
you want to stay with Flo . . . that really is a
. . . a knife in the bosom. And if that was all
you had to say to me, poppet, I can't imagine
why you had to drag me here at this ungodly
hour to listen.

AUNTIE. Mrs. Beresford is wheeling her aunt
down to the pawnbrokers. Old habits die hard.
H.P. for the youngsters; uncle for the ever-
greens. . . . Is that all?

MIRIAM. If I expected consideration, I must have
been out of my mind. But why should Flo be
favored?

AUNTIE. I may be wangled out of my home, but I've
no intention of giving up everything that makes
life worth living.

MIRIAM. I should have thought staying with Flo was
a fate worse than death. Lunches of yogurt and
nuts.

AUNTIE. You know my hobby. I study human beings.
Humans are more varied, and less predictable
than butterflies. I keep my collection in this
diary. Wherever I go, this diary goes with me.
Do you see daylight yet?

MIRIAM. No, Auntie.

AUNTIE. When I'm locked away from the world, I'll
only have a few people to work on. For my own
convenience, I would rather start with Florence
and her brood.

MIRIAM. Ah!

AUNTIE. At the end of six months, I should have a
    very full diary.

MIRIAM. I can imagine it. Absolutely absorbing.

AUNTIE. You may as well understand from the
    start, Miriam, that I find it almost impossible
    to carry on a sane conversation with you. What
    shall I do when you and I are confined for six
    months?

MIRIAM. I don't think that's altogether funny,
    Auntie.

AUNTIE. But there's one topic of conversation
    which I can always renew, and you'll never
    exhaust. Florence.

MIRIAM. Florence.

AUNTIE. Mention any hour of any day, and I'll tell
    you waht happened then. It will all be in my
    diary. What time of morning Wilfred tiptoes
    home and what is said over breakfast afterward.

MIRIAM. Darling!

AUNTIE. How long the grocery bills run unpaid.

MIRIAM. Precious!

AUNTIE. And where the surplus housekeeping funds
    are invested.

MIRIAM. Sweetie!

AUNTIE. What Florence does in the long winter
    evenings will help to pass our long summer days.
    You don't mind, now, if I visit Florence first?

MIRIAM. But just a moment . . . how can you find
    out all that if you never leave your room?

AUNTIE. I never leave this room, but I can tell you
    that you bought a model hat last Thursday.

MIRIAM. I didn't!

AUNTIE. A purple creation from Buxbies. Very
    expensive.

MIRIAM. That's not true. I mean, it was a mistake.
    I mean, it's only on approval.

AUNTIE. That means you haven't told George yet.

MIRIAM. He's so obstinate. Particularly about
    hats.
AUNTIE. You see? . . . Florence has a telephone.
MIRIAM. Who hasn't.
AUNTIE. And a couple of little beasts who'd be a
    credit to any terrorist organization. Yes, I'll
    have my fun with Florence.
MIRIAM. What about me, Auntie?
AUNTIE. I'll have even more fun with you, Miriam.
    That is, if I ever come to stay.
MIRIAM. You shall. You shall. I insist.
AUNTIE. But Florence first.
MIRIAM. Florence first. And to hell with the Costa
    Brava.
AUNTIE. Now run away. I have work to do, even if
    you haven't. What have you done with the twins?
MIRIAM. They're at school, dear. You forget how
    time flies. In any case, if I ever leave them
    alone, I only have to slip them sixpence, and
    they're as good as gold. They'll do anything for
    sixpence.
AUNTIE. That's useful. Good-bye, Miriam.
MIRIAM. Oh . . . you . . . er . . . won't tell
    George about the hat, will you?
AUNTIE. Not a word. I promise.
MIRIAM. I hate George to worry. I'm soft-hearted
    that way. Bye-bye, Auntie, love. (She goes
    out and shuts the door.)
AUNTIE (looking down into the street). Ten-fifty.
    Mr. and Mrs. Knee walk arm in arm toward the
    town. Mrs. Knee has a discolored eye, but
    otherwise appears satisfied. . . . It works like
    a machine. You put your penny in, and . . .

(The lights are lowered to denote the passing of time.
    When the lights are raised, FLORENCE is seen
    pacing up and down.)

FLO. A simple answer to a simple question --
      that's all I ask. Why Miriam this morning?
AUNTIE. You've seen her?
FLO. She agreed with me.
AUNTIE. That sounds serious.
FLO. Now what am I to do?
AUNTIE. Exactly as you please.
FLO. My principle has always been -- contradict
      Miriam, and you can't go far wrong. As long
      as she insisted on having you first, I knew
      where I stood. But now . . . I'm baffled.
AUNTIE. You could change your mind, too, and
      bundle me off to Miriam first.
FLO. But suppose that's what she really wants,
      and this is an underhand way of getting it.
      Whatever I do, I'm likely to be cheated.
      Imagine -- double-crossed by that bubble
      brain. But the scheme isn't hers.
AUNTIE. She handled her cards very well. She
      surprised me.
FLO. Tell me . . . what does Miriam know?
AUNTIE. You'd better ask her.
FLO. I want to know now.
AUNTIE. Then ask her now. She must be halfway
      up the stairs.
FLO. How do you know?
AUNTIE. My window. I saw her running across the
      road. And I'll tell you this much, Florence.
      Miriam isn't happy, either.

          (MIRIAM hurtles into room.)

MIRIAM. Ah! I thought so.
AUNTIE. You're soon back, Miriam, dear.
MIRIAM. Don't you call me dear, Auntie, darling.
      That's hypocrisy. What are you doing with Flo?
FLO. Florence is trying to discover what you have

been up to with Auntie.

MIRIAM. It's all a plot. A wicked plot.

FLO. Open of you to admit it.

MIRIAM. Can't you see, Flo?

FLO. All I can see is my sister, flapping around
like a demented duck.

MIRIAM. You needn't crow; she's done it to you,
too. She's driven a wedge.

FLO. A what?

MIRIAM. A wedge. You know what a wedge is,
don't you?

FLO. Of course I know what a wedge is.

MIRIAM. Well, she's driven it. Once we're
divided, she can twist us around her . . . her
bedpost. Her and her diary.

FLO. What diary?

MIRIAM. You know perfectly well what diary,
sweetikins. The diary Auntie has just been
telling you about. Oh, yes, Auntie, dear, the
whole scheme's as clear as a . . . a search-
light. The twins would do anything for sixpence.
Who will be paying them? It all adds up.
There'll be a diary about me, too. Something
to keep Florence amused during the long winter
evenings.

FLO. I said -- what diary?

MIRIAM. Drop the innocent air, Flo, darling. It
doesn't deceive me, and only makes you look
retarded. There's been only one diary mentioned today . . . the topic of conversation for
a six-month stretch. You can't deny it. What
else were you talking about when I caught you
here?

FLO. You. And I repeat -- what diary?

AUNTIE. If you hadn't run, Miriam, you might have
given yourself time to think. . . . (Looks down
into the street.) Mr. Balsam is buying a

pineapple. (Writes in diary.) "Mr. Balsam
buys pineapple. "

FLO. Auntie's diary?

AUNTIE (writing). "Flo notices diary. "

FLO. You, too. That means me, too. Too. Too.
Too.

MIRIAM. For goodness sake, stop plonking away
on one word.

FLO. Why am I to look after Auntie first?

MIRIAM. I have a generous disposition. Obviously,
you wanted Auntie first. Take her, angel, with
my blessing.

FLO. Her diary. Her diary includes me, too. Ah!

MIRIAM. Stop thinking. You're wrong. Absolutely
wrong.

FLO. Ah!

MIRIAM. That's merely the perverted way your
mind works. As if I'd have a flicker of interest
in Auntie's diary.

FLO. Ah!

MIRIAM. Let my brother-in-law come home when-
ever he chooses. And why should I concern
myself with your grocery bills?

FLO. Ah!

MIRIAM. In any case, why shouldn't I find out what
goes on behind your curtains? For six months
afterward you'll be ferreting out what goes on
behind mine.

FLO. Ah!

MIRIAM. Don't keep honking like a diesel engine.
It's driving me mad.

FLO. You surprise me, Miriam. Yes, after all
these years, you've managed to surprise me.
Congratulations. I thought I'd anticipated the
worst. Sisters ought to watch out for double-
crossing, back-biting, and the occasional
confidence trick. A sister can't sink lower than

that. I thought. I was mistaken. My sister
proposes to plant a spy in my own home.

MIRIAM. Don't mention scruples to me, darling.

FLO. I never mentioned scruples.

MIRIAM. I doubt if you know what scruples are.

FLO. I have scruples.

MIRIAM. How amazing. You actually have scruples,
darling.

FLO. I have scruples to spare.

MIRIAM. What do you mean by scruples?

FLO. I mean scruples. Do you?

AUNTIE. There's no call for a megaphone. When
Florence is finished with me, I go to Miriam.
When Miriam is tired, I return to Florence.
You each have a go in turn. What does it matter
which square you start from? Why not toss for
it? Heads or tails makes no real difference.

MIRIAM. I have a sentimental nature. It's always
being abused.

FLO. We'll stick to our agreement. Auntie comes
to me first.

AUNTIE. Noble of you, Florence.

FLO. But she won't keep a diary.

AUNTIE. A diary isn't essential. I have a memory.

FLO. Meaning?

AUNTIE. What were you doing at three in the afternoon a fortnight ago last Thursday?

FLO. Me? Nothing. What am I supposed to have
done?

AUNTIE. Shall I remind you in front of Miriam?

FLO. No!

MIRIAM. Auntie, dearest, you shouldn't do that to
me -- offer a tidbit and then snatch it away.

AUNTIE. Would the word salmon mean anything to
you, Miriam?

MIRIAM. Auntie!

AUNTIE. I'm not boasting, mind -- merely stating

facts. I'm fond of facts. I collect them. As
long as I'm at your elbow, the information is
available. You can have it for the asking.

MIRIAM. Can we?

AUNTIE. And as long as information is available,
you'll be asking for it.

MIRIAM. You make me feel so helpless, dear.

FLO. Nicely tempted, Auntie. But there is an
answer.

AUNTIE. What?

FLO. Self-restraint.

AUNTIE. Sell that to Miriam.

FLO. If neither of us asks, neither of us will find
out. That way we're safe. Agreed? Of course
it is; you can't do anything else.

AUNTIE. Do you agree, Miriam?

FLO. You'd better.

AUNTIE. You don't want to know what George said
when he opened a certain parcel by mistake?

FLO. No, thank you.

AUNTIE. You don't want to know how Wilfred
sprained his ankle after last New Year's ball?

MIRIAM. Well . . .

FLO. Don't give way, Miriam. We'll support each
other like Alcoholics Anonymous. When you feel
like reaching for another slice of scandal, give
a ring. I'll drop everything and calm you down.

MIRIAM. But what happens when you're tempted,
darling?

FLO. I have strength of character. You have to
trust me.

AUNTIE. There's the answer. Trust each other.

MIRIAM. It won't work.

FLO. It must.

MIRIAM. I can stick my fingers in my ears when-
ever Auntie drops a hint. I can cross my heart
when I swear I never asked the slightest question.

But you won't believe me.

FLO. How do you know I won't believe you?

MIRIAM. Because I won't believe you, either.

FLO. Are you calling me a liar?

MIRIAM. Of course, darling. You're my sister.
Trust you, Flo? I'd sooner trust a ravening
octopus. No, our lives will be public property
as long as we have Auntie on our doorsteps.

AUNTIE. I wondered how long you'd take to get
there.

MIRIAM. So, every six months there'll be fresh
revelations. It will be like having an earth-
quake twice a year -- exciting in its way, but
inconvenient in the long run.

FLO. There is an answer.

MIRIAM. I know what you're about to say, darling,
but don't let that stop you saying it.

FLO. One of us must keep Auntie all the time.

MIRIAM. Exactly.

FLO. I said "one of us."

MIRIAM. It was a noble suggestion. You were
speaking for yourself, of course.

FLO. Auntie, you'll roast in hell for this.

AUNTIE. Not only this. (Thumps on the floor.)

FLO. What was that for?

AUNTIE. Bring Louie up.

FLO. I don't want Louie.

AUNTIE. That month's notice has to be canceled.

MIRIAM. Cancel the notice? But the double rent,
darling.

AUNTIE. You wouldn't have your old Auntie on the
streets?

FLO. You had this fiasco all arranged from the
start.

AUNTIE. You arranged it with Miriam. My dears,
you're as free as air. You name the game, I'll
play it.

(Enter LOUISE.)

AUNTIE. But you must both be very kind to Louise;
    she was so looking forward to losing me.
LOUISE. What does that mean?
AUNTIE. What it says. But don't let that alter your
    plans. The place could do with a spring clean.
LOUISE. Florence! Miriam!
MIRIAM. Why should you worry, darling? At
    least you can look forward to your rent.
LOUISE. I won't be made a fool of. I . . . I'll take steps.
FLO. Take my advice instead. Don't. . . . Have
    you quite finished with us, Auntie?
AUNTIE. Do call again.
FLO. Not this year. Coming, Miriam?
MIRIAM. Auntie, dear, you've been absolutely
    beastly, but I forgive you. I have a forgiving
    nature. I'll be back next week. Then you can
    tell me all about . . .
FLO. Miriam! (She seizes MIRIAM by the arm and
    begins to drag her out.)
MIRIAM. Florence! (The door slams behind them.)
LOUISE. Of all the underhand . . .
AUNTIE. They changed their minds. It's allowed.
    It's a pity to abuse their charitable instincts,
    though. You won't raise the rent, will you?
LOUISE. I'll do whatever I like. You've no hold on me.
AUNTIE. Hold? Do you take me for an all-in
    wrestler? . . . Still, next time you're at The
    Cormorant Club . . .
LOUISE. I've never been near The Cormorant Club.
AUNTIE. No, but next time you're there . . .

(The door opens and BETTY hurries in.)

BETTY. Sorry to keep you, but . . . oh, Miss
    Louise. You came up.

LOUISE. I came up.

AUNTIE. While you're here, Betty, You may as well run across to the sweetshop for me. Can she, Louie?

LOUISE. Do whatever you like. Who owns this business, anyway? (She goes out, slamming the door behind her.)

BETTY. What's with her?

AUNTIE. She's human. It takes some getting used to. Now, what's all this about Charlie?

BETTY. His name's Percy, and I think we click.

AUNTIE. He was supposed to be Charlie.

BETTY. Some of us have minds of our own. What do you want from the sweetshop?

AUNTIE. Do you like chlorodyne gums?

BETTY. No.

AUNTIE. Chlorodyne gums, then.

BETTY. You call it manipulation, don't you? Well, you can chew this with your chlorodyne gums -- you can only manipulate people who let you manipulate them.

AUNTIE. That's a lot of words.

BETTY. A quarter?

AUNTIE. Two ounces.

BETTY. Right.

AUNTIE. And, Betty . . .

BETTY. Yes?

AUNTIE. You stick to that.

BETTY. You bet. (She goes out.)

AUNTIE. It makes a change . . . (Looks down into the street.) Mr. and Mrs. Scan walking toward town with the three Scan boys. They look a happy family. That worked smoothly enough. . . . All the same, it makes a change.

CURTAIN

PROPERTIES

NOTE:
The action takes place in Auntie's room over-looking a busy street. The lights are lowered to denote time lapses between the four scenes, but as no redressing of the stage is necessary, there should be no long waits at these points.

GENERAL PROPERTIES:
A bed with a bookcase headboard; a locker; two chairs; a telephone; a large window.

PERSONAL PROPERTIES:
AUNTIE: A pair of binoculars, a large book, a pen, a stick.
FLORENCE: A bag of green grapes.
MIRIAM: A couple of peaches.
BETTY. A bag of peppermints.

DIRECTOR'S NOTES

DIRECTOR'S NOTES